Gnashing Teeth Publishing
242 East Main Street
Norman AR 71960
http://GnashingTeethPublishing.com

Printed in the United States of America

ISBN 978-1-966075-09-7

Non-Fiction: Poetry

Gnashing Teeth Publishing First Edition

PERIODIC ELEMENTS

by

Georgia San Li

Always, For JKJ

TABLE OF CONTENTS

"...As if this earth in fast thick pants were breathing,
A mighty fountain momently was forced:
Amid whose swift half-intermitted burst
Huge fragments vaulted like rebounding hail,
Or chaffy grain beneath the thresher's flail:
And 'mid these dancing rocks at once and ever
It flung up momently the sacred river...."

Kubla Khan
Or a Vision in a Dream. A Fragment
by Samuel Taylor Coleridge

PART ONE   *Water*

The exodus of young men

from South Korea / after the war / second sons like my father / from *yangban* houses / who fulfilled their military duties / then left for America / for their futures / with their intellects / with ambitions and philosophies of life / they chose /from the choices they had / and he / chose to start his family at Eagle Heights / not far /from my birthplace / not far /from University Hospital / where I have returned/ to my future / my American heartland / in a white rental / white / the Korean color of grief / it is more visible in hazardous skies / and now I remember / how he loved to fish in these lakes / and I imagine schools/ of perch / swimming to old Bayside for hundreds of years amid spotted cows / harkening home /to the canton of Glarus, / once Ennenda / Netstal and Riedern / schools of perch /their whirring /clasped/ under my ribs / as if caged in the Earth / in its heavy / aged ice / I grip the wheel quaking / holding my yearning for the ocean / in great swells / suddenly / they flood my limbs / pinch my feet and ankles / swollen with generations past / whom my father brought over oceans in exodus / the inevitable reformation along wild grasses / fields of corn and barley /where warm chestnut trees once stood in dusk like this

listening for history / poetry / and literature / in memories of my father along pastures and traces / whirring quietly / whirring home / this land amid cherry orchards /and milk

Early Definition, circa 1977

Are you Chinese? Are
you Japanese? my
classmates clamored out

from the playground, walking
home from Mrs. Benasek's
second grade room, asking

unable to locate my
origin, and from somewhere
I saw an Eskimo, how clever

more intriguing, a human mystery
no one would have guessed it
soft kitten-fur framing

frostbitten cheeks, my pearls of
happy teeth, over-dressed
in the ¾- sleeve glitter blue

dress my mother made from
what had caught my eye in
the remnant rack at

Parkway Plaza, the dress
for the first day of school
shimmering in the winterless

gleaming sunshine, drifts of
snow moving in clouds, memory
of my aggrieved mother

watching Omar
Sharif in a fur hat, Dr.
Zhivago, riding a horse-drawn

carriage with Lara, how lovely
Lara, that woman's face in love
that woman, not my mother

The Red Clay Court

take the wood racket
he places in your hand, its gut strings

vibrating with the thump
of a flat shot (no slices

no drops), connecting with his
tennis ball somewhere in the soft

sweet middle, firm and strong, your
left knees bends low, your grip on

green tape carries your power through
a full backhand swing of imagination and form –

a natural angle that does not twist
the elbow, forcing movement

your tennis shoes, gritty red clay
take the shape of wings dusting

the baseline, waiting for the long shots
you believed you could win, none of them

impossible to get until he proved to
you his power was in wingspan

life played across the full court –
give me your best shot
make your move –
let's play

Martin & Eckmann Clothiers store, Seattle, 1955

What Becomes of Us

Not your favorite wire glasses for reading
the newspapers delivered to your porch

Not the walks to Peet's Coffee before
picking up cage-free eggs, fresh tomatoes
and camembert if you were in the mood

Not the Mathematical Handbook for
Scientists and Engineers your advisor gave you

Not the money you made at Martin & Eckmann's
for rent of your room at the boarding house

Not your cheering for Jimmy Connors because
he was the underdog
playing McEnroe that day

Not the French movies with Catherine Deneuve
or Gérard Depardieu
nor the telenovela soap we watched you watching
after you stopped wandering the world

Not the short story you wrote about a $5 dollar bill
named Richard

Not even when you sang *non, je ne regret rien* for us
and Jeni played the piano

I kept, of course, the baptism certificate dated June 4th, 1958, found
in your briefcase, but I don't know
what it means anymore
        And when she called the pastor
        as though you needed salvation, I glanced at her
        primly because I am well-trained

Not your night sweats and delirium, not even when the two of us
were on walkie-talkies in case you needed me
and I hear your voice upstairs whispering
Sorry to wake you

Waking

I have no clairvoyant wisdom
though clarity sparkles
waiting unhurried imagining
his face made of clouds in another emerald
lit galaxy that will withdraw into darkness
with the moon I can barely see

puzzle pieces on a mobile
in my mind, silent and spinning:
   his camel trench
coat, his hands
   in his pockets, a box
of lemon
        drops he loved
butterscotch
          ice cream, Christmas
    for the children
the turmoil of religion, belief, and will
another perspective create
a Jurassic world of giant echinacea
along fescue grass on canvas to hang
over the mantle   Should I put my shoes
on to leave, walk into the day
from this imagination and memory
where he lives with me
I want another day, every day
like this, creating new time
by the oceans, its foam kissing my hair
searching, for his existence
and staving off, one more time
another tidal wave of sorrow
I hold in my breath
as if this is my greatest
possession, as if this will
in the end be enough

To love the earth

know its thick coat of
winter, its frosty courage
borne by its Achilles heel of love

to lean on in shaping the emptiness
from a strong footing against
the ice floes breaking apart

over an egg harbor safeguarding
the schools of perch learning to
speak, their little mouths mimicking

their mothers, writing songs in
perfumes of the invisible water until
spring ushers them into inlets and

scrawls of the rivers to finally wrest
fifty years from bended knee

PART TWO   *Fire*

A Strand

A strand extrudes from a kernel
of utterance, snapping to far reaches
as if a power of truth lies in its key
signature, a fantasie impromptu

passing through your creature-hood
its viaducts, your breaths transcribing
imagination into diction, strung
in C# sequences like DNA, into folds

agitato, a complex of emotions
and coming to terms in so vying
to capture variable, random
combinations of happenings, elapsing

with time into a form of definition
that slips away through cracks, like broken
egg, as if it never existed, but watch: it delves
for human nature by the throat

Forkprints

pressed against copper reveal
patterns of fossilized flowers mixed with

mud-cracked seeds, pebbling rocks
of brown barley, red beans, smashed

leaving imprints against char-riddled
rice, scraped and singed at the bottom of her

copper pan, panning gold, but *aiyishii*
there is nothing, nothing

burning bright in the cruel bubbling rivers of
indelible summer heat she slurps before

she sets the table, and knows not what to call this
American alien mixture of no lilacs, no

tubers, with no redemption in
their eyes

Spectacle

we found the photo on
his phone, a violent train
track from the base

of his neck to his sacrum
melded with red macadam
snipped ends of wire

whiskers; his blue johnny
laid opened like stage curtains
bunched under his arms

so she could better see, take a
photo using his camera
stifle her sudden gasp of awe

awakening to something
amazing, how could this be
his torso cut open in half –

put back together, she dared
not touch the seam, re-open
the cage that held her heart;

she hated that he had to try
so hard to love her

Americana on Oak Tree Drive

Charlie Brown, *I waited for you*!
my little sister Sally cried before I
cared that I was big brother enough
to be bossy I left her crying under
the school flagpole because
our mother arrived late, walking
from our ranch house on Oak Tree Drive
in plastic green sandals with heels made
of cork that could float like a bottle over
the ocean but ruined her feet

I waited for her too, standing on the yellow
paint lines watching new friends play
with a tetherball as round as my head, hitting
it hard, wrapping rope around a metal pipe
It is 1971 when we ride in the backseat
of my father's Dodge Valiant, leaving
summers swum in Pine Lake eating
peanut butter and jam soaked in Wonder
Bread in the rain

Gold-rim glasses framed my sister Sally's
face. She read Harriet the Spy in the closet
while I organized battalions of army men
with David (P.) and David (F.)
Sliding on our bellies, we trained for war
at eye level in our backyard

We made use of the dry dirt under vines
tomato that fell like *bombs away* Or hid
behind zucchini for the spaghetti he taught
our mother to make from a Betty Crocker
cookbook which she read, mostly guessing
because she did not understand English
It is the year Nixon was elected President
a man walked on the Moon, Walter Cronkite
reporting "That's the way it is," smiling as
if there was nothing wrong in the world

Soon our parents hosted weekend dinner parties
our mother made cream puffs with Cool Whip
craving steamed mochi stuffed with sweet bean paste
that her mother's housekeeper made before
the war, before the rubble

왜 왔어?
Wei-whats-uh?

Why come this far? And when my father asked
why four bedrooms are not enough
she cited scripture: *your children are raised
by a wife more precious than rubies*

We saw Lucy and Linus at reunions
our parents moved to a two-story
white stucco after we left
for college They were still married when
forty-five years later states struck down bans
on gay marriage, over 200 countries
commit to reducing use of fossil fuels to
preserve the Earth

That spring our father smiled like a masked
astronaut through bubbled glass

또왔어?
Tto-whats-uh?

You came again? His eyes talk to me as he sets
down his briefcase at the front door
his day of work done His hand squeezes mine

I squeeze back twice to tell him he is
entering the rooms of my childhood, holding
my hand because I have nothing to fear

He is home, our mother softly snoring, her
mouth agape, and Sally and I are both beside him, still
crying in silence We did not wish to wake her
immovable in her belief, she had always done what was
right She had given him everything, made spaghetti
out of nothing: this was the kind of wife she was

Undoing

like slabs of fog, frozen in icy allusions
burrowing deep into dark

pine forests, brimming with fiery red sun
stark black needles bristling in a shadow

play of knives, inflammable tinder
skin that sheds its cells of broken mirrors

her pointed finger
injecting alignment, respect

for her lofty brothers and sisters, darkening
golden daylight streaming through the window

blinds you hold still again for a moment
a state of numb-skulled waiting to be over

for a taste of affection to materialize –
Would anyone recognize the phantom

sandcastle, its shambles, its cuneiform
even if love is what it still wants
to be?

No Escape Plan

It took only one perfectly blue
morning in September to lose living
in my sweet pudgy life, in a new nest

for the three of us along an arbor
lane, a choir of mythic yellow
chrysanthemums heralding my arrival

like giant trumpets bursting
out of magic mulch which my young
mother when she was heavily pregnant

with me shoveled into a wheelbarrow
from a heap on a neighbor's
driveway from across the cul-de-sac

Twin swords rose like a mirage
out of a moon called New
York, attacked using imploding

machines setting fire with gases
destruction, made into utter powder
by terror in the name

of reclamation and royalty Not knowing
which symbols of power would turn into dust
people poured out of offices on Summer

Street, afraid to look over their shoulders
But I could not hear her: *How will we find you?*
Who would take you as their own?

Synapses

If everything revolves
as expected, run away, call out

to those lurking two-eyed
sockets, faces starched open

in ohs of astonishment, watching
for spectacle from every corner

from base boards and drywall
Drain energy from the very

depths of their invisible copper
mesh, wasps burring, conducting electricity

along each crevice of spine and
vestigial tail, perforating porous space

between my ears, electrify
tiny neurons in search of just one

small key to relief from nullity, let
imagination fall like love, let me

drink its terrible iridescence
as if from a poisoned chalice, let it

burn through the back of my throat
let it rush open the prison gates

Dol-lim Ja Imprints
characters for the next generation

One generation of heirloom tomatoes divide their eggs
       bubbling with blisters, bloody
       broken stems in the end
How many precious pigeon-red rubies will man
       flood with fires and
       vengeance of war in the end?
Who were the three African women
       in tangerine silks and golden slippers
       rerouted at Charles De Gaulle again in the end?
A telecom engineer died of a heart attack at Novatel
       blue body flown to Texas
       on the company plane, cargo in the end
Would salarymen eat bowls of ramen with
       tonkatsu and bamboo shoots
       in subway stations at Aoyama in the end?
How long did the security caravan of Range Rovers
       maneuver over dunes before
       locating the lost daughter in the end?
She ate alone in Mayfair, shriveling in a black pant suit
       tandoo-ri chicken and its charcoaled skin
       pinot grigio in the end
In naming the unborn grandson, only he heard
       the noemic rush-hour traffic
       roods over rooftops outside his window in the end
Did Fernando de la Rosa hide guns with the dulce de leche
       for Christmas, blue-blazered foreigners
       at Benito Juárez airport in the end?
After dinner in the medina, sprigs of sugary dates await you
       but beastly brooding, desert sky
       swallows you whole in the end
Would the Internet of Things learn to dance
       become human chanteuse
       discover the meaning of star-beds in the end?
Along the green gushing river entering Sao Paulo
       would shanty towns shout
       studded with hailstones in the end?
When my grandfather named me, devastation grew
       rooted in the character for one, for unique, for singular —
       fault lines, all breaking open in the end

As if there were only science

once upon a time
a child undeserved

of suffering now
looks at the hooks of

hostility, pyrrhic victories
searches for causalities

of origin and in this more
massive sphere, finding

nothing of heaven, only
human body, an amalgam

sacs bustling with
cytoplasm holding irresistible

forces of biology, its
demands, you think

I can pick and choose
what applies

this empirical nose, this ear
this personality and character

these wormy apples
for your basket

encoded and correct
as if there were nothing in

the nucleus, nothing you want
delicately to perfect

as if there were nothing
without annihilating it all

"…CD said human consciousness shows up in the
record as symbolic behavior toward the dead…"

Consciousness by Robert Hass

In the morning void after years

since my father died, opening my eyes,
the moment seems a slit of air between sliding glass
doors into the backyard patio, a blear of
red marigolds and eucalyptus I could sense
her refulgent mood, then my vision apprehends
the tall window covered in fine mesh to redirect
her ultraviolet radiation, a pinky orange jewel
exuding a deepening breath of fire
day breaking as if time were nothing

As I rest my eyes, close them behind warm
translucent skin, my mind leaps forward in search
of the dreamy joy that has darted away It is
daughterhood I think of, playing hide and seek
under leaves of verdant hostas
Such dreams must thrive in partial sun —
akin to the daughterhood of Cordelia?
Both my hands pull and pluck at her
back, grab a piece of her empire-cut gown
but she evaporates into whiteness and
her snapping flicker of poetry eludes me She hides
still alive, not dead, somewhere where I can no longer
retrieve particulars, only an empty sense
of rupture I begin to wake, imagining white noise
absorbed by the white alabaster walls and the sheets
The dragon tree on the dresser stands stoic
unwilling to complain of the environment
next to the tv, a dark polaroid, coated in dust
with no aspect to develop, still and present in
its situated darkness

I sit up and watch the plane ascending
shearing open invisible streams of wind A circle
of seagulls keeps its distance, Cordelia
rushes past their ears, before subsumed, slipping
into the stratosphere Looking over the
brightening horizon, I remember the politics
of the waste processing plant on Deer Island
Little remains of its nature Strange nothing is yet burning

A Sunday afternoon in the city
rolls from a tape of square stickers

a honeycomb of Tinkerbells, sweet
remnants from a time when her pudgy

fingers posed under her chin and
laughed at the funny world, when

she called me Aurora, no longer Sleeping
Beauty, no longer playful animation, no

make-believe cartoon illusions on the park
bench in the greenway, by the blue bike

stands, no squinting smiles hovering over
red courthouses etched with governing

words, after the scarring, spoken
aloud by Martin Luther King, a drape

of curtain like a heavy mural by our own
Diego Rivera drawing our gaze to a flock

of futurist air balloons, painted over
graffiti in red

in red
balloons, a bouquet of hot teardrops

in somersault, floating across concrete
chutes and wrought-iron ladders

salty soup dripping over rooflines, greasy
windowsills, crusted with dirt

and sand, eyes
blinded

blind fear of lost used-to-be
what might be outside

these eyes never looking up
never washed in the rain

PART THREE *Wind*

There, its many different roads
of tangled red petals flutter
along bougainvillea, thick and heavy
over years of reaching
along the roof line, a cantilever of
wet black boughs lifting drenched memories
out of stormy rains: her father's
scientific journals, his gray Samsonite
briefcase, rustling ribbons of perforated
computer paper, scratch papers, blue-lined
yellow tablets scribbled with pen and
penciled equations of ideas, symbols
seeking to solve the problem of
proof of existence in shapes of chestnut
wood, smoothed and spherical, resonant with sweet
smoke of his father's tobacco, beads of
an old abacus clackity-clacking
stirring sounds of his father's study aglow with moon
gleams, butterfly-petals dance on white paper walls:
there, across the mullions, pages
of his pocketbook calendars flutter, unfolding

Untitled: a portrait from the tarmac

Take down your dancing shoes
slip them on your youthful mind
looking up into the sunset, empty

skies filling your eyes with vision
No one walks along the road of life
with you now, so, you whistle an

old folksong talking to that stranger
you remember who, when you landed
at Chicago O'Hare on that Pan Am

flight in 1964, emerged from the crowd
after waiting behind the chain-linked
fence—at once a noble creature

re-render the marble torso under his
white button-down dress shirt, the stroke
of a brow line, from the side

his handsome earlobe, his shining black hair
whisked by the windy city You play
with this fire, yank at your throbbing heart

no longer a stranger, now that these
skies are empty though this ambition and
hopes are still tangling and burn

into knots — at least now let us
dance, let me call you *dahngshin*, let me
see you forever in front of my eyes

More in September

For DP & MP

one morning we thought of
the more we write construing
this more in slow lightning
      slow light and what is more –
      more release, more content more
      nonsense into more
discovery more invention
more unfolding gently hidden joys
more adventure more bursts
      of starry-eyed delight more still
      trees along the block we are
      walking on Erie after lime
lemonade in September to
celebrate healing more in writing
memoir in the aftermath of
      his wife's infidelity with a
      man in Morocco more walking
      to-and-fro' more waving
at a Subaru you thought
was your husband but it was red
not blue under shadows
      by the streetlamp more he
      dashed from work with no
      time to eat more to be with you
after all day in emergencies
more grasping your hand in
the heat more gulps of water
      more you learn reporters would
      rather make friends and read
      poetry and write about how
technology affects our lives
because they have to more
punctuated conversation in
      the humidity of night more in this
      clean well-lit space near MIT
      under the steep staircase more
chandelier of broken plates
and cups and saucers
suspended in the shape of
      a tulip upside down more calling
      our friend in Washington DC from
      the street on the spur of a wish

Where are the frog poems?

Where in the jut-lands and promontory
        blocking the summer solstice
its invisible face still magnifying
    shadows still falling after evening talks
after questions are met with answers
        as last bits of pineapple and jalapeño are
swallowed, where did he point to? There
        are frog poems out there! that poet declared
unreserved, holding time in abeyance
        striding past, leaving his well-worn
overcoat behind, and dismissing the
        coming frost, his thick blue-gray cotton
garb draped over his body like the hoary
        skin of a bear, he perhaps seeking to
remain incognito, the brim of his hat
        pressed over white brows of gentle
consternation and reproof at us for idling
        though we notice his arm held high, his
finger still pointing, hovering in the air
        perhaps somehow detecting
along the most sensitive patterns of his
        fingerprint the quality of sheen
permeating the valley with the scent of its
        ambiance, the kind of sound that lifts
the weight of the earth, formed of a veil
        of molecules containing underestimated
power, sheen that softens
        the greedy unmitigated wants and
ambitions fueling can't you see? your
        blindness, your incorrigible attempts to
reach some sort of beauty along an
        unnecessarily narrow road for naught —

Oh là là where are the frog poems out
        there, each silent with sounds mimicking the
snow melt traveling from broad-shouldered
        granite peaks, making its way through
the marshy foreground, its sounds opening
        the embouchure and filling its body
venting its cryptic curves, its dewy
        bejeweled back emerging with dreams
made of moonlight meeting the sun, while its
        sticky toes grasp cedar in a

waltz in the light heart that whirs around
     him, that poet, with sound of play and
whirling wind —
     Oh là là the whirl to jump
from, to plunge from and begin—

PART FOUR *Earth*

Epitome, *She*

After shocks rage
after years contained in this
middle-aged celadon overfull of
revolt and revolution from Earth

who took this gentle man,
from *geum san li*, a long ago
lost village, now seeking not
knowledge, but understanding in

fluttering lines of narration – come
Raven, wrestling shape without form
squinting through lashes, aiming to
create some sort of mechanical

clarification, blow glassy heart
and sinew as breaths arise surrounding
your mind, clouds in your ears
straining wheat from husks, until

interrupted, noticing the surrounding
and power of jet engines
at 30000 feet propelling
time forward over Her adamant

ruts and roads and allusions to
humpback whales and woolly
mammoths, such ancient beasts
such religion, the She who determined

His whatness, when, and why and held
dominion over it all —

O cunning Love! with tears thou keep'st me blind,
Lest eyes well-seeing thy foul faults should find.

Sonnet 148
William Shakespeare

Admonishment

How will you contain
    this tumbling trajectory

into a handkerchief?
    What words will fill

this basket for fruit
    without rotting — *sohk sahng hae*

Where will you plant the
    crumpled paper to grow

with the trees? If only it were
    seed that bore poetry

When will you stop seeking
    vengeance for your father's exile into

your mother's realm of righteousness?
    How will you stop the crackling

of branches burning unless you
    put down your pen:

Your father is dead When you look
    in the mirror, who will you see?

Your mother
    Your father

Periodic Elements

As rust and mineral
deposits scorch

their residues onto the morning
hot water pot

it still whistles
set with too many various

buttons as if I should be
attentive to chemistry, even slight

alterations in temperatures
molecular weight, and

concentration that would
modify solution from liquid to

vapors, as if periodic elements
we are made of

could not penetrate
stainless steel

At moonset from Boston Harbor
for my father – on our walk tonight, let's take the long way home

I heard the warbling of October, *adieu*
        your soft opalescence of hope along

the slope of the Okura
        its fine serenity made of impossibly

steep hills, narrow paths of timeless tradition and
                ceremony, Old Tokyo never sleeping –

The neon lights of Roppongi give way
        thrust into an array of sunlight

its temple bells, its utter calm and fragility
                accompanying the street sweepers

who emerge from subway tunnels
        and unmarked doors, donning

crisp blue jackets, and clean white gloves
                who sweep the storefronts spotless –

sweep the high-heeled boot prints
        the glittered streets

Gall & Game

knowing the foundations
of ignorance, spent
in and out of big and
small turmoils and frustrations
minor and major horrors
obsolescence and obtacles
over crusts and canyons
accumulating like
subcutaneous fats
and marrow, spread over
toast like jam, insoluble, in
need of apple vinegar and
chai to quench and metabolize energy
through systems and neurology:

chance is its instant impulse
hesitation, guts and possibility

decisions to make or say
nothing or something that

flits away, disappearing –
lightning bugs, under leafage

of enchanted night, already
forgotten

PART FIVE   *Space*

One Thousand Years from Behind Us

Would there be ocean, crescent valleys of
      grain, birds of prey circling
Flower farms for bees and honey
      preserved in civilization, its burr and
Blades of helicopters made of glass bodies
      for camouflage in chase in the foothills
Training for war, deemed done for a state of
      readiness, distrustful and unyielding
Delineating decorum and sovereignty with
      budgets from taxes, still in trade for plastics
Would the animals collected and born into
      captivity as phenomena watch us
In fear, in quietude, every day and every
      night as we keep them
Faces gazing askance, wondering how
      their lives had come to this
Under siege of fire and brimstone storming
      south under the rage of red sun
Would nitrogen and oxygen drift through
      the moon-sphere and cool their nostrils
Would the Earth be volatile, tempestuous
      bone cold
Would there be luminosity from the galaxy
      from depths of sea, of golden kelp beds
Where seals and otters play at the cove
      in breaks of light
Would this be how the animals understood
      freedom, their bodies permeated
Accustomed to isolation, to enclosures
      Would there be anyone left to decide to
Live life in some other way, to discover one
      thousand years from behind us the
Mountain is higher, past what we could see —
      what would children left there think?

Inchon Airport at 5 am

giant neon halos hang
from the ceiling/over a row of lanky young trees

in white high tops/ their verdant hair styles
both brushed: unbrushed/

in a poised: natural stance/ swaying
to the right/ with the look of abandonment: happiness

like those K-Pop boy bands, their wisps of eyeshadow
and blush/ powdered innocence: powdered swank, on Tik Tok

dancing/ the Tik Tok of remaking themselves before
dawn breaks/ over the Shilla at the base of

Namsan mountain/ where the spirits of Obon rush
past them/ along the festival, the Tik Tok parades/ghosts/

those angelic faces, Tik Tok/ never to be children

Ellipsis

Aren't we all strangers by nature/ all
poets/using picks & shovels/ to excavate memory/
for revelations we only detect/ if we realize/ a moment

of lightning/ hold up/the candelabra
to the music/ even as you curl / on your bed
in the figure of a tender furled fern/

alveoli popping /like heads/ of white cauliflowers
blooming/ into marble/are you wishing
for your lover /to knock

open /the screen window/and climb in /through
your memories/ as you watch/ eyes blink/
in your reflection on the phone/ propped /against

the pillow you hug / holding/ your last breaths
like long kisses/while blue / balloons glow / in new ideas
and emojis/something true on the horizon

over the comforter/would what you see /be
the ellipsis/thrumming/someone/in the amphitheater/
wanting to reach the high notes/ revising the ballad/backstage/

thinking of you/that face watching your reflection
/blinking/your thinking eyes/see the doe / at
the window / waiting /for the last message:

Crystalline & Amorphous Solids

tsundoku defies logic, a library
of mordant moorings, books
you collect strewn & stacked

into an object of desire to enter a gateway
and invite disturbance, texta by texta
an understanding that senses

the marred driftwood dissolving
into silts of gurgling sulfur, cradled
in lunar craters of pink

iridescence, all that is left of white retroscape
that was once flush with the gush of wild
rivers, throngs of goldfish

as limestone and chaparral mark
the perimeter, and the margins grow
blank with meaning, margins of space

an irascible octopus with spotted
architecture, who defends herself
by disappearing

Notes

Early Definition, circa 1977, is a work of memory, from its own remnant rack of desire and love and yearning to come alive again. It began from a retrospective on the question of origin, of revelations from metaphor, its DNA. It laments what it cannot forget — a love, it realizes, might have never existed. It was strange to find snow on return to the desert sun, carrying images of a woman's face from circa 1977. The time frame, unreliable.

"What Becomes of Us" grew out of reading the poem "What Belongs to Us" by the poet Marie Howe.

Each stanza of the poem "Dol-lim Ja Imprints" describes a scene from life and memory. In ancient Korean tradition, a *dollimja* character is used to identify members of a clan who are in the same generation. See, e.g. http://en.wikipedia.org/wiki/Korean_name.

"One Thousand Years from Behind Us" emerged after a reading and lecture given by Forrest Gander at the 2023 Community of Writers poetry conference citing an essay titled 'The Possibilities Of Poetry: On 'Be With' By Forrest Gander, Lotte L.S. , September 23rd, 2018 08:44; see https://thequietus.com/articles/25352-be-with-forrest-gander-review ("..Aymara is the only studied culture for which the past is linguistically and conceptually in front of its speakers, while the future lies behind them.")

Acknowledgements

Grateful acknowledgment is made to the editors of the following imprints and journals where poems in this manuscript first appeared, sometimes in earlier forms and under different titles:

The exodus of young men – selected for the 2023 Oxford Poetry Prize shortlist (Nov 2023), first published by The Missouri Review (Jan 2024)

Early Definition, circa 1977 – The Interpreter's House (UK) (Nov 2024)

Forkprints – Cathexis Northwest Press (2023 January – February)

Spectacle, One Thousand Years from Behind Us, Inchon Airport at 5 am – The Glacier (Dec 2023)

Americana on Oak Tree Drive – Willow Springs (Spring 2024, Issue 93)

Dol-lim Ja Imprints – selected for the 2023 Oxford Poetry Prize shortlist (Nov), first published by Heavy Feather Review (Feb 2024)

As if there were only science; Epitome, *She* – Ravensperch (Nov 2023)

In the morning void after years; At moonset from Boston Harbor – Rising Phoenix Review (Nov 2023)

A Sunday afternoon in the city – Emerge Literary Journal (October 2023, Issue 28)

There, its many different roads – The Dawntreader (UK) (Spring 2024, Issue 66)

More in September – formerly titled "The Full Report," Exposition Review (July 2024); nominated for Best of the Net, the Nancy Riggs Poetry Award and Pushcart Prize

Where are the frog poems? – Pembroke Magazine (Summer 2024)

Ellipsis – POET LORE (Summer/Fall 2024)

Crystalline & Amorphous Solids – selected for the 2024 The London Magazine Poetry Prize longlist; first published by Blackbox Manifold (July 2024)

The author wishes to extend special thanks to Finishing Line Press as the publisher of *Wandering*, her first chapbook (FLP 2024), where these poems appeared:
>   The exodus of young men, To love the earth, Forkprints, Americana on Oak Tree Drive, Untitled: portrait from the tarmac

Special thanks to Karen Cline-Tardiff and the team at Gnashing Teeth Publishing for selecting this book for publication and making the dream of this book a reality.

About the Author

Georgia San Li is the author of Wandering, a Minerva Rising finalist and published by Finishing Line Press (2024), and Intermezzo, forthcoming from Ravenna Press. Her poems were longlisted for the 2024 London Magazine Poetry Prize and other poetry was shortlisted for the 2023 Oxford Poetry Prize. Her chapbook arrangement of Small Galaxies for Breakfast was a semifinalist for the 2024 Tomaž Šalamun Prize. Her poems have been nominated for the 2025 Pushcart Prize. She lives and writes in New England.

Praise for *Periodic Elements*

The first thing one notices about *Periodic Elements*, is the predominance of simple, tight forms, with many poems composed of couplets and tercets. The second thing one notices, though, is how unexpectedly these forms are constructed. Form and content push and pull in restless kinesis, giving the sense that meaning is seeking simultaneously to both inhabit and escape from the lines on the page. And this, of course, is what these poems are all about – locations and dislocations, connections and disconnections, the everyday and the abstract, not as discrete experiences, but as the volatile and inseparable admixture of opposites which fuel our lives. Alive with restless contradictions which, viewed as a whole, cohere into precise new shapes on every reading, the third thing one might notice about *Periodic Elements* is that there are no full stops...

Oz Hardwick, author of *A Census of Preconceptions*

The poems in Georgia San Li's *Periodic Elements* offer what I most wish for from a poetry collection: a bridge between the senses' observable realism and a more speculative realm of mind and soul. In vibrant sinuous sentences, San Li juggles the intersection of science and literature, from Korean tradition to American pop culture to the broader embrace of global intellectual thought. It's a stunning performance.

Dave King, author of *The Ha-Ha*

A luminous, philosophical exploration of family, identity, and the natural world. Diverse and playful in form, the poems are grounded in fresh, vivid imagery, full of earthly delights. Georgia San Li's collection takes readers on a journey of both aching nostalgia and momentum questing forward.

Amanda Quaid, author of *No Obvious Distress*

The poems in Georgia San Li's marvelous book reward a reader with their ample, vivid description, and through that description, the poet reveals the greater mosaic of the past. These poems aim to make sense of the past—make meaning from a personal history—and the act of remembering as captured in these rich and alluring poems is the essential work of poetry. Georgia San Li is a poet of great gifts, and *Periodic Elements* is the proof.

Mark Wunderlich, author of *God of Nothingness*

www.ingramcontent.com/pod-product-compliance
Lightning Source LLC
Chambersburg PA
CBHW041153120626
46547CB00020B/3200